CW00568097

Alison · Kinnaird
∴ THE · SMALL · HARP ∴
A Step By Step Tutor

KINMOR MUSIC
SHILLINGHILL, TEMPLE, MIDLOTHIAN, SCOTLAND

ISBN 0 9511204 2 5

Music Copyright

Thanks to Bob Groat and John Sinclair for allowing me to arrange their compositions **Balfour Village** [No. 21] and **The Shapinsay Polka** [No. 22] – published Shapinsay Community Council.

To Patersons Publishing Co. for permission to arrange **Queen Elizabeth's March** by Pipe Major W. Ross [No. 15].

To Alan Reid for allowing me to arrange the **Islay Jig** [No. 19] – published Kinmor Music.

Acknowledgements

To Joyce McMillan for patiently typing all the information in the book.

To Isobel Mieras for advice and help with proof reading.

And to Robin.

INTRODUCTION

This book is an introduction to the small harp, or clarsach. I have aimed it at two main groups of players. First, the complete beginner, who is perhaps not able to get to a teacher easily, if at all, and who may or may not be able to read music. Second, those players who have been taught classical harp music but who are interested in the tradition of Scottish and Irish music and would like to know how to approach it. As well as these two groups I hope that any harp player may simply enjoy playing the tunes that I have chosen.

My own interest is in traditional music so the tunes have been arranged in traditional style. The basic technique may be similar for both the traditional player and the concert harpist, but good traditional style demands some special techniques of its own. In particular, a guide to grace-notes and ornamentation is given in the book.

If you want to play Scottish or Irish music on the small harp, in the end you have to use informed musical judgement about the quality of the music you are playing. As I see it, a traditional style is the best way to express the music because of its national character and the continuity of its historical roots. It is also the best way to bring out the unique dignity of the clarsach as an instrument in its own right. It is not just a small, beginner's harp.

Equally, to see traditional music as "small" classical music shows a lack of true understanding of music. I find this as unsatisfactory as the performance of folk songs by opera singers. It may sound pretty - they are usually good tunes! - but it has nothing to do with our countries' rich heritage of language, native song and instrumental traditions. My favourite quote on the subject comes from Joseph Elouis, a classical harpist, who was originally Swiss but lived for many years in Edinburgh. Commenting on the classical style arrangements of Scottish music which were fashionable in the 19th century, he says "That neither talents nor ingenuity can render such Accompaniments compatible with the Scottish Airs is strongly exemplified by those of the great Composer Haydn, which although replete with merit, give no idea of Scottish music: and for that reason, may be compared to a portrait exquisitely painted but deficient in resemblance".

My own style of arrangement has grown naturally and gradually from familiarity with the way the music is treated on the other instruments used in the Scottish and Irish traditions. Listening to other good musicians is the only way to acquire an ear for this. As the harping tradition was broken at the end of the 18th century in both Scotland and Ireland, my music does not attempt to reconstruct this lost music but to fit into traditional music as it is played and sung today - a progression which is what one would expect in the natural flow of a continuous tradition.

The arrangements may appear "simple" at first sight. I choose not to use many harmony notes at a time, preferring to let the ringing nature of the instrument carry the harmonies through. I aim for harmonic transparency and clarity of the melodic line. Do not be misled into assuming that these are all beginners' tunes! In the first place one of the most difficult things is to play a melody well. But also, if you are not familiar with traditional style, the music demands a certain amount of understanding and commitment if it is to be played fluently and convincingly. It is rather like acquiring another language. After the basic sequence of elementary lessons, the tunes are not arranged in a particular order though they do tend to become rather more advanced as the book progresses.

The tunes are not, on the whole, melodies which were composed for the harp, except for some compositions of my own. But they have been chosen because they suit the instrument - they bring out the character of the clarsach, and they come easily to the fingers. Also, they are good tunes! If you are interested in actual harp tunes you can refer to my earlier book **"The Harp Key"** which is a collection of tunes composed for, or linked with, the Scottish harp from the 17th century to the present day.

I have thought carefully about how to present the music in the most accessible way and this book is the result of more than fifteen years of teaching, both individual pupils and in groups, with a good deal of experimentation on my part. I normally now teach mostly orally and find that the results are very encouraging. As one American student said to me "I have never learned a tune so quickly or so well". The accompanying tape will take the beginner from the first steps of tuning the harp through the elementary lessons. I also demonstrate the decoration exercises and give a lesson on playing one of the tunes which uses these ornamentations. A guide to musical notation is also included but I hope that the combination of recorded and printed music will also encourage those players who do not read music to explore and to enjoy the instrument.

One does not, after all, need to read music to play it. Some of the finest musicians I know do not read a note. It is far more important to listen - music is sound.

There are many varying approaches to playing the small harp. The one I present here is my own. But I have learned a great deal from the approaches of other teachers like Isobel Mieras, Anne Macdearmid and Sanchia Pielou, and from each of my pupils over the years, some of whom are now themselves teaching. I would like to thank them all, and to express the satisfaction and optimism that I am sure we all feel in the growth of interest that has taken place over the past few years in this delightful and important instrument.

Alison Kinnaird
1989

USING THE CASSETTE

I recorded the cassette which accompanies this book because it is often much easier to play something if you have first heard it demonstrated. Before you listen to the cassette, read the introductory section on "Beginning To Play", and keep checking with the written instructions as you go along. Whether you read music or not, use the printed page as a reference for fingering and setting instructions. It is impossible to demonstrate hand position and fingering visually, as one would normally do when teaching orally, so use the diagrams and written instructions in conjunction with the cassette. If you do not read music this is a good way to begin to read it because you can follow the printed notes along with the way they sound on the tape.

The beginners' exercises and tunes contained in the Lessons are all demonstrated. The tunes are played quite deliberately and clearly in order for you to hear exactly what is going on. You should stop the tape at the end of each Lesson, and should not progress to the next stage until you feel quite comfortable with the part that you are working on. Work at your own speed.

At the end of the tape I give a complete lesson based on a more advanced tune. I chose this tune because it demonstrates a good range of the grace-notes, and also shows the subtleties of timing which are impossible to write down.

The Harp or Clarsach – the names are used interchangeably throughout the book.

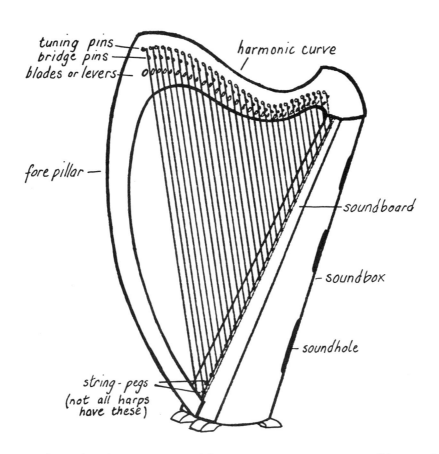

The clarsach is a simply constructed instrument. The shape will vary from maker to maker, as will the design of the semitone blades or levers which raise the pitch of each string a semitone by pressing against the string to shorten it by an exact amount.

Buying an Instrument

The two main criteria for an instrument are that it should have a good tone and that it should be reliably constructed. The tensions within a fully strung harp are considerable, and it is not unknown for a badly made instrument to pull itself apart. There should be a full and even tone from bass to treble strings, and there should be no rattles or buzzes when each string is played. The semitone blades or levers should be checked individually to make sure they are accurate and firm. They should be exactly in tune, and should not slip out or buzz if the string is plucked hard. The tuning pins should be firm but easy to turn a very slight amount – fine tuning is all that is normally necessary. If you have any choice, I would not advise buying a harp with less than three octaves range (this is a knee harp) unless you want it for a particular purpose. Four or more octaves are necessary if you are not to be limited in the music you can tackle. I would also advise against buying a harp without semitone blades or levers – this will require a lot more tuning from key to key, and is a disadvantage for a beginner. Harps may have gut or nylon strings. I prefer the sound of gut but nylon has some advantages in extreme climates. Gut strings react more to temperature and humidity, and tend to become sharp in the cold, and flatten when the atmosphere is hot or humid because the gut absorbs moisture more than the nylon does. The Clarsach Society and many harp makers run a harp hire scheme so that you can try an instrument without the expense of buying one. This is definitely worth considering.

MAINTAINING YOUR HARP

It is important that your clarsach should be well made so that it will not give you trouble because it warps, twists or cracks due to poor construction or badly prepared wood.

However it is up to you to look after it well. Even the best made harps cannot deal with bad conditions. Here are some rules and tips you can follow.

1. Keep the clarsach in an even temperature as far as possible. Wide variation in temperature is bad for the wood and will make it very difficult to keep in tune.

2. Keep the humidity, also, as even as possible. Damp will affect gut-strung harps particularly badly.

3. Do not place your harp near a central heating radiator or any other source of heat. These can be switched on unexpectedly and do irreparable damage.

4. Do not leave your harp in full sunlight.

5. Place your harp somewhere where it will not be knocked or bumped against. They are not very stable instruments and falling over is one of the main causes of damage.

6. Keep your clarsach fully strung. If a string breaks, replace it as soon as possible. If you cannot replace it immediately, cut the broken string off, leaving the end in place close to the little peg which holds it in the sound box. This means that the peg will not fall out and get lost before you get the chance to put a new string on.

7. Always keep your harp in tune. There are considerable strains on the body of the harp, and if the pull of the strings is not kept constant, these stresses can change.

8. Make sure that the right gauge of string is used. Each harp is made to take a particular thickness of string and too thick or too thin a string will not have good tone. It is a good idea to keep a selection of strings (at least 2 or 3 from each octave) with you at all times when you are playing.

9. In emergencies, red or black waterproof felt-tip pens can be used to give you a string of the right colour. Make sure they are waterproof and indelible or you will end up with colour all over your strings and fingers!

10. If a string is slipping when you tune it up, first check that it is winding up away from the end of the tuning pin. If they wind towards the end of the pin they eventually keep falling over the end as you wind it up. If the tuning pin itself is slipping, you can tap it gently right out, tapping with a small hammer on the end which has the string hole in it. You can then dust the pin with grated resin and re-insert it. This, surprisingly, also makes pins which tend to stick turn more easily. A few harps have screw-thread tuning pins. These should not be hammered in or out. It is unlikely that they will slip, but you should make sure that any threaded tuning pins are screwed right back until the string hole is near the wood before a new string is inserted. Otherwise they just screw themselves further and further through. Look up the section on stringing a harp for detailed instructions about putting on a new string.

11. Protect the blades or levers from being knocked. They are the most vulnerable point on the harp and it is very common for them to be broken off, especially the bottom one. If you are putting the clarsach flat in a car or van for transport, make sure it is not resting on the levers and that they are suitably padded if anything else is laid on top.

12. A case of some sort is essential if you are transporting the harp anywhere. These can be soft, padded or fibreglass, depending on the conditions of travel.

13. Several people have asked whether to slacken their strings when taking the harp in an aircraft. With today's conditions of flight I have never found any need to do this but, if you are concerned about your harp, they may be slackened by a semi-tone. Do not slacken them completely. This would not be good for the harp - it would upset the tensions in it.

14. If your blades or levers are not tight against the string when tuned, (and in a well-made harp they should be good and firm on the string) you can try wrapping a piece of thick tape round a loose blade or glueing on a small piece of thin leather. However, these are emergency measures only, not a solution to the problem.

15. If your blades screw directly into the wood and are too tight, try taking them right out of the harp, rubbing the screw thread with a little candle wax or graphite and screwing them carefully back in again.

16. If your blades screw directly into the wood and are too loose, so that they tend to slip out if you play that note hard or often, you can try taking them out of the harp and either putting a few drops of methylated spirits into the hole, or wrapping a piece of thread round the screw before replacing them carefully. Both of these are effective short-term measures.

17. If a plastic or metal lever is damaged or broken, contact the harp maker as soon as possible for a replacement. These can usually be reasonably simply fitted.

18. If your harp is buzzing, check that the levers or blades are not touching any of the strings. It is not necessarily the one you are playing. Check that none of the levers or blades are loose. Check that none of the strings are fraying. If one is one is developing "whiskers", you need to replace it immediately. Check that the pegs in the sound box are firm. Check inside the harp in case the knotted end of one of the strings is touching the back of the sound board. Check that the harp is firmly on the floor or stool - not rattling on it. Check that no buttons, zips or jewellery on your clothing are vibrating against the harp. Kilt pins are bad for this. Check that the screws holding the feet on are not loose.
If none of these solve the problem, see an instrument repairer.

REPLACING A STRING

It is essential that your clarsach is kept fully strung and in tune at all times. If a string breaks, you must replace it with one of the correct gauge. Most harp makers or good music shops which sell harps can supply one. The strings are usually numbered from the top, but each harp may have a different number of strings so it is a good idea to get one of the supplier's lists of strings and work out which will fit your own harp. You must keep a gut-strung harp strung with gut strings, and nylon for a nylon strung harp. The difference in tone is considerable.

1. When you have got the correct string ready, remove the little peg on the sound board and the ends of the old string. Some harps don't use the pegs and just have a knot at the back of the sound board.

2. Prepare the new string by tying a large knot at the end. Some people tie the thin strings round a little piece of thick string to make the knot firm. The main thing is that it should not slip through the hole in the sound board. The piece of thick string is essential if you have no pegs.

3. Thread a felt washer down the string till it rests on the knot. If you don't have felt washers, don't worry, they are optional.

4. Thread the unknotted end of the string through the sound holes in the back of the clarsach till the end comes through the little empty hole in the sound board. Pull it gently through till you feel the knot at the back of the sound board.
   Some harps have sound-holes too small to get your hand into the box. With these it is necessary to thread the lower end of the string through from the front of the sound-box before you knot the string. Knot it when it appears through the sound-hole, then pull it back by the unknotted end till the knot holds firm inside the clarsach.

5. Replace the peg on the front of the sound board. Push it in firmly. Make sure, if it has a little groove in one side, that this is against the string.

6. Bring the unknotted end up and thread it through the hole in the tuning pin. Make sure the string is on the correct side of your levers and bridge-pins. Don't pull it too tight at this point, leave just a little "give" in it.

7. Begin to turn the tuning-pin with your key. Check that the string is still on the correct side of the levers and bridge-pin. Check that the string is winding towards the harp, not towards the end of the tuning-pin, or it may slip off before you get it tight enough.

8. Check that the peg in the sound board is still firmly in place.

9. Tune the string up slowly and steadily. Check how the note is rising against the other strings that are in tune. Bring it up to pitch, and a little sharp, because the string will immediately stretch quite a lot and will continue to go flat until it settles. Keep tuning it up gradually.

10. Cut the long end off neatly above the tuning pin.

11. Avoid doing this just before you have to perform, unless it is an emergency!

TUNING YOUR CLARSACH

I tune my clarsach in the key of C, with no sharps or flats, as do many of the players who concentrate on traditional music. Many other players, however, tune their harps in E^b, which has three flats. You must make a decision for yourself as to whether you would find it useful to tune in E^b. However, for the purposes of this book I would advise beginners to tune in C.

There are pros and cons for each key.

C - Advantages

1. Most traditional tunes are written or were composed in sharp keys. Transposing them changes their character. I know that modern pitch has changed since many were written, but I am going by common usage nowadays, not making an antiquarian reconstruction of the music.

2. If you want to learn them in a key in which you could play with other instruments, e.g. fiddle or whistle, you should learn them in the sharp keys in which they are originally set. Playing along with other instrumentalists is one of the great pleasures of traditional music.

3. The fewer blades or levers you need to use the better. You do not have to turn as many blades or levers to reach the sharp keys. The more levers you use the more you lose tone. Also, levers on many harps are unreliable or inaccurate, especially if you are playing loudly.

4. C is a good beginners' key. Your 'doh' note is a red string so it is easy to find.

C - Disadvantages

1. You need to tune a string down a semi-tone if you need a flat.

E^b - Advantages

1. You are unlikely to need more than 3 flats at any point.

2. Singers like the flat keys and the variety this gives them.

E^b - Disadvantages

1. You have to put in at least 3 levers to reach the sharp keys, with resulting loss of tone and problems with reliability and accuracy.

2. If you want to play with other people, the flat keys are not popular with other instrumentalists. If you have learned a tune in a flat key, they may not be able to play along.

I should point out that E^b was chosen as the tuning key, purely arbitrarily, at the end of the 19th century. It could just as well have been A^b which was chosen, which would give you 4 flats. Up until the end of the 18th century the old system of tuning was quite unlike the modern classical system, and included two strings in the middle of the harp (the "sisters") tuned to the same note.

Tuning in C

The other reason why I choose to tune in C is that it is easy for beginners.

> Your red strings are C.
> Your black strings are F.

So your 'doh' note – C – is a red string. The harp is tuned in a diatonic scale, i.e. doh-re-mi-fa-soh-lah-te-doh.

If you do not have a piano or electronic tuner, you can tune the harp to itself, but it is always a good idea to check it against concert pitch every few days to make sure it is not drifting badly sharp or flat. If you are playing with other instruments, of course, it is essential to remain in concert pitch.

Tune the middle octave first. Start with C. Then tune in 5ths and 4ths upwards until you have tuned one octave. Thus C up to G, G down to D, D up to A, A down to E, E up to B, B down to F, F up to C. Then tune in octaves, up and down the harp. Always play the note that you know is in tune first – i.e. the one you have just tuned – because your ear automatically assumes that the note it hears first is correct. Tuning will gradually become easier as your ear gets accustomed to the intervals.

Your harp is now tuned in C. If you wish to tune in E^b, follow the same procedure starting tuning with the middle E^b string, tuning upwards in 5ths and 4ths. Thus – E^b up to B^b, B^b down to F, F up to C, etc.

Blades or Levers

The clarsach can be put into other keys by turning the blades or levers that press against the top of each string. These sharpen the string by a semitone. Thus, putting in the F blades will give you a scale of G, etc. The blades or levers are put in in the following patterns to achieve the desired key.

> If your harp is tuned in E^b
>
> For the key of B^b – turn A blades
> F   – turn A and E blades
> C   – turn A, E, and B blades
>
> If your harp is tuned in C
>
> For the key of G – turn F blades
> D   – turn F and C blades
> A   – turn F, C, and G blades
> E   – turn F, C, G and D blades

Obviously if you are tuning in E^b you will continue turning blades in the same pattern when your harp reaches C if you want to use the sharp keys.

I have set all the beginner's tunes in C. Where it is necessary to put in blades or levers, I indicate this at the start of the tune, giving the correct blades for both tunings.

When you have finished playing, remember to take off any blades or levers. They put an extra strain on the string so they should not be left on when the harp is not being used.

HOW TO READ MUSIC

A Basic Guide

Musical notation is simply a code by which music can be written down. It may look complicated but the basic principles are quite straight forward.

1. Music is written on a pattern of 5 lines and spaces. This is called the "staff".

2. The music has two elements – Pitch and Rhythm. Pitch is written up and down on the staff (vertically). Rhythm is written along the staff (horizontally).

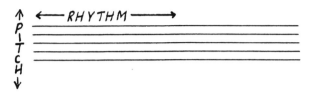

Pitch

3. Clefs – On the clarsach we have both high – treble – and low – bass – (pronounced "base") notes. The high notes, usually played on the right hand, are represented by a sign called a treble clef at the beginning of the staff.

    The low notes, usually played by the left hand, are shown by a bass clef at the beginning of the staff.

4. The notes are given letters as names. We use seven letters, A – G. So ABCDEFGABCDEFGABC etc. From one A to the next A is an octave (8 notes) so is B to the next B, C to the next C, etc.

5. On the staff each line or space represents a particular note.

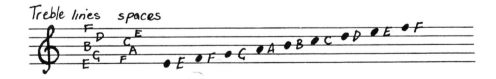

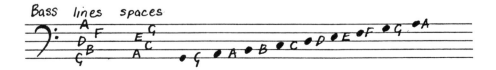

6. You can see that there are not enough lines and spaces to fit all the notes on the harp so notes which are higher or lower than the staff have a little section of line drawn especially for them. These are called ledger lines.

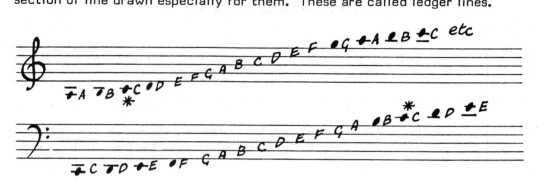

7. The note with the star * is middle C. It falls between the treble clef and bass clef where they overlap. Each harp may have a different number of strings but, roughly speaking, middle C will be the middle red string on your harp.

Sharps and Flats

8. The smallest distance between two notes in classical music is called a semi-tone. A tone is made up of two semi-tones.

    You can make each note on your harp a semi-tone higher by turning the blades or levers so that they press against the string.

9. The sign for a note which has been raised a semi-tone is a sharp. #

    So C with a sharp sign in front of it is played half a tone higher – C#.

    F with a sharp sign in front of it is played half a tone higher – F#.

10. The sign for a note which has been lowered a semi-tone is a flat. So B with a flat sign in front of it is played half a tone lower – B♭.

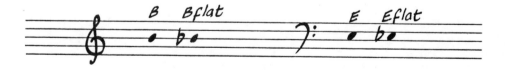

    A natural sign restores the note to its original pitch. ♮

13.

11. Sometimes a note is intended to be played a semi-tone sharp or flat for a short time only. Then the sharp or flat sign will be written in front of that note, rather than at the beginning of the staff. This is known as an accidental and lasts for only one bar or measure of the music (see 17. Time Signature – bars).

12. A scale is composed of tones and semi-tones.

     doh   re   me   fah   so   lah   te   doh
       tone   tone semi-tone   tone   tone   tone semi-tone

All major scales have this pattern of tones and semi-tones – the semi-tones occur between the 3rd and 4th notes, and between the 7th and 8th notes.

Key.

13. To have C always as your 'doh' note – that is to play always in the key of C major – would be very boring. We can change the 'doh' note to any other note but the pattern of tones and semi-tones must remain the same if you are to play a major scale starting on that note. You must therefore use your blades or levers to give you the necessary semi-tones.

To save writing sharps or flats all through the music the sharps or flats you need are written on the appropriate lines at the beginning of the staff. This is called the key signature.

Thus   Key of C
              no sharps or flats

            Key of G
            1 sharp (F♯)
            C tuning – turn all F blades or levers

            Key of D
            2 sharps (F♯ and C♯)
            C tuning – turn all F and C blades or levers

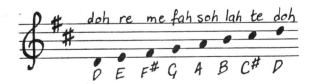

If you tune your harp in E^b, your 'doh' note is E^b.

Thus

Key of E^b
3 flats (A^b, E^b, and B^b)
E^b tuning – no levers

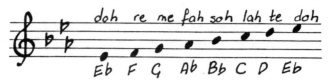

Key of B^b
2 flats (E^b and B^b)
E^b tuning – turn all A levers

Key of F
1 flat (B^b)
E^b tuning – turn all A and E levers

In E^b tuning, to reach the key of C, which has no flats or sharps, you must turn all the A, E and B levers. From this point, to reach the sharp keys of G, D, etc., follow the pattern as given for C tuning. So, for the key of G, a harp with E^b tuning will need to turn all the A, E, B and F levers. For the key of D you would need all A, E, B, F and C levers. (This is why I prefer to tune my clarsach in C!).

14. At the start of each tune I have written the levers you will need. However, the pattern of blades for each key should be memorised as soon as possible.

Again, any extra sharp or flat notes which occur in the music will be written in individually as an 'accidental' and last for one bar only. I have indicated in the music where to turn the appropriate lever with the left hand – and where to turn it back.

15. When your clarsach is set in each key you can play a <u>minor</u> scale as well as a major one. The 'doh' note for a minor scale is a third (3 notes counting the one you are on) below the major 'doh' note. So the relative minor to G is E minor and the relative minor to D is B minor, etc. Try out the scale you can play if you start on the minor 'doh' note. It sounds quite different from the major scale – I always think it sounds sad compared with it.

Rhythm

16. Note Values

When you listen to music you are aware of a steady throb or pulse. Perhaps it is because we are constantly accompanied by our own heartbeat that we need to define music in this way or indeed any regular sound, like the tick-tock of a clock.

The pulses or <u>beats</u> are written thus.

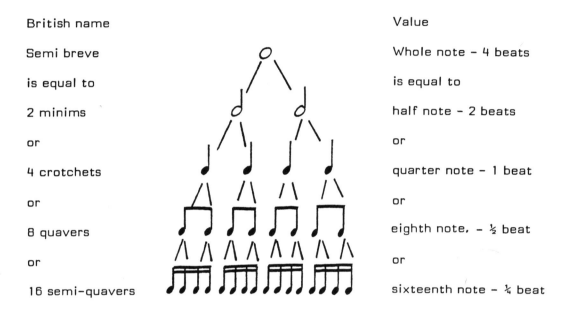

British name		Value
Semi breve		Whole note – 4 beats
is equal to		is equal to
2 minims		half note – 2 beats
or		or
4 crotchets		quarter note – 1 beat
or		or
8 quavers		eighth note, – ½ beat
or		or
16 semi-quavers		sixteenth note – ¼ beat

Dots after a note indicate they have the extra value of half of the preceding beat.

Triplets

Sometimes notes are placed in a bar so that they do not quite fit the regular count. A bracket and a number above the notes concerned tell you that three notes must fit into the time normally taken by two.

17. Time Signature

At intervals in a pulse there is a stronger beat or accent, e.g. oom-pa-pa, oom pa-pa, or tick-tock, tick-tock. The number of beats between these accents divide the music into bars, with the accent coming at the beginning of each bar. After the bass or treble clef we write two numbers which tell us the number of beats in a bar, and which note represents one beat.

E.g. 2 3 6   The upper number tells you how many beats in a bar.
     2 4 8   The lower number tells you which note represents one beat.

So you could write tick-tock as

2 beats in bar   2 beats in bar   2 beats in bar
minim (½ note) = 1 beat   crotchet (¼ note) = 1 beat   quaver (eighth note) = 1 beat

Or oom-pa-pa as

3 beats in bar   3 beats in bar   3 beats in bar

½ note or minim   ¼ note or crotchet   eighth note or quaver
= 1 beat   = 1 beat   = 1 beat

The most common tune signatures used in traditional music are

4 crotchets in a bar   

3 crotchets in a bar   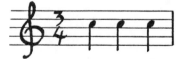

6 quavers in a bar   

9 quavers in a bar.   

When you count out a tune you count the rhythm as a series of regular syllables.

So 4
    4

Say it aloud

18. To divide the rhythm we count it as "one-and", two-and", etc., or dividing
     it further - "o-one-and-a", "two-oo-and-a", etc. Keep the count regular.

Try tapping out these rhythms as you count them aloud. Keep them steady.

19. Rests

     The silences in music are as important as the notes. They are represented thus:

Semibreve	𝅝	=	▬	
Minim	𝅗𝅥	=	▬	
Crotchet	♩	=	𝄽	or 𝄾
Quaver	♪	=	𝄾	
Semiquaver	𝅘𝅥𝅯	=	𝄿	
Dotted notes work the same way	♩.	=	𝄽.	

20. Some commonly used signs

♩_♪ A tie between two notes indicates that they should be played as one.

⌢ A Pause – above a note means it may last as long as the player wishes.

‖ Double bars indicate the end of a part.

‖: :‖ Repeat sign indicates that the part should be repeated.

Brackets mean that the bars within the bracket marked "1st" are played first time through the tune. The bars marked "2nd" are played on the repeat.

⌐— 1st ———⌐   ⌐— 2nd ———⌐

{ Beside a chord indicates that the chord should be broken, i.e. played from the bottom note upwards, very fast.

{ Indicates the chord should be broken downwards, starting from the top note.

3 ⌒ 1
1 ⌣ 3   A tie mark on fingering indicates that the finger should cross over or under.

1 ⌁ 1   A straight line between fingering indicates that the thumb should slide.

⌐——⌐
1 2 3   A bracket over a group of fingering means that all these notes may be set in place at once.

LH   Means Left Hand.

RH   Means Right Hand.

In general, I have written the notes with tails up for the right hand, tails down for the left hand.

FINE means FINISH. So when you are repeating part of a tune you finish at this point.

D.C. al FINE means repeat the tune from the beginning (Da Capo) to where you see FINE.

D.S. al FINE means repeat the tune from the sign (usually '𝄋.) to where you see FINE.

BEGINNING TO PLAY

Sitting

This may sound fairly obvious but is is very important that you sit comfortably at your harp - or you will not want to spend time with it.

Since the length of everyone's back is different, and so are the harps, here are some guidelines.

Your back should be straight. This will avoid "traditional" back trouble in later years!

The harp should rest comfortably on your right shoulder, without danger of it falling forward, or feeling that it is pushing you back. You should not need to hold on to it. In the old days wire strung harps were played on the left shoulder. Almost all harps are now made to be played on the right. You can then reach the blades or levers with the left hand.

The harp should lean back at an angle so that the strings are more or less perpendicular to the ground. This makes it easier to get your fingers between them.

You can sit at whatever level you feel comfortable. Some people sit on stools, some kneel, with the harp on the floor, some sit on chairs with the harp on a stand or stool, and some stand, with the harp higher still. The important thing is that it should be steady. I would recommend sitting astride the harp, either on a stool, or on a chair with the harp raised on a stand or stool. Your feet should be evenly on the floor.

Back

Your back must also be straight to avoid tension. This must be avoided right down the arms from neck to fingertips.

Neck

Relax the muscles between the neck and shoulder.

Shoulders

Drop the shoulders till they are completely relaxed. Never hunch them forward. You will create tensions in neck and arms, and will also tend to play inwards, not projecting the music.

Left Upper Arm

You will be playing mainly at the top of the harp with the right hand, and at the bottom with the left hand. But it is important that the left hand is able to swing upward to reach the treble strings when necessary. Your left elbow must therefore be at a level from which your lower arm can reach both the lowest and highest notes with the minimum movement. Your shoulder should not have to move at all, and certainly should not pull up towards your ear. All the work should be done below the elbow. It is not necessary to hold the elbows as high as for the concert harp player – they have further to reach on the larger instrument.

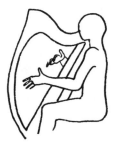

Left Forearm and Wrist

Do not get into the habit of playing with your elbow on your knee! The forearm must have free movement at all times. Hold the arm up about the centre of the harp with your palm down. The wrist should be straight between your knuckles and your elbow. It should remain basically straight all the time you play. It must not bend down, or up, as this will bring your fingers to the strings at the wrong angle. It will also put strain on the carpal nerves in your wrist.

Right Arm

This arm is not expected to reach the bottom strings because your harp is in the way! It must be able to reach the top two or three octaves easily. I find it best to rest my forearm lightly on the box of the harp, with the elbow about nine or ten inches out from my side. It should not be clamped down to your side, nor is it necessary to hold it out at 90°. Free, comfortable movement is what you are looking for. Again your wrist should be straight from elbow to knuckles.

You may have to adjust the level of your elbow slightly depending on the width of your sound-box.

Hands

Fingers are numbered Thumb = 1, Fingers = 2, 3 and 4. The little finger is never used. The hand position is rather unexpected. Most people think clarsach players waft their hands gracefully around the instrument, but of course one is actually looking for a strong, safe touch on the harp which will get the best tone and accuracy. The position is basically the same for both hands.

21.

Thumb Positions

Start with your palms down, fingers and thumbs extended together. Bend your fingers only down at 90° to your arm.

Raise your thumb behind the hand. Touch your knuckles with the joint of the thumb. Get the feel of this position. Move it about 1" away from the hand. Place the thumb, still in this position, on a C string. You will notice that the thumb covers a relatively large area of string because it is touching it at angle, not straight on.

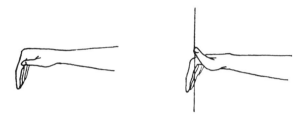

We do not play straight on to the strings because you would catch your nails on them, and because the large amount of string one is able to pluck with the pad of the finger gives a full, warm tone. Pluck the string by moving the thumb towards the knuckles to touch the first joint of the finger. The thumbs may bend over the top of the fingers as they touch. Always pluck with the side of the thumb.

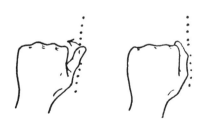

Repeat this movement until it becomes comfortable. Arms, wrist and the rest of the hand should have remained basically in the same position. Try not to let them get tense. Do not pull your hand back away from the harp. You want to keep your hands close to the strings. It avoids unnecessary work moving them back to the strings after each pluck.

FINGERS - 2nd Finger

With elbows, wrists and knuckles in a straight line, palms down, thumb on string as described above, and fingers bent down from knuckles at 90°, extend 2nd finger forwards till it has the B string running up the centre of the pad, again at a long angle. Pluck the string down and inwards so that your finger ends up in your palm. The other fingers will follow it in sympathy. Relax and let them do so. Practise 1 2, 1 2, 1 2 until it is comfortable. Do the work with fingers only. Put each finger back before you play the next finger. It gives you something to pull against.

When you are used to the feel of working with these two fingers, you may like to try the exercises and tunes in Lesson One.

3rd Finger

Follow the same procedure - 1 onto C, 2 on B. Extend the 3rd finger till it is safely on the A string. Again a long angle of string will cross the side of the finger pad. Pluck down into the palm. Fingers bend up till they touch the palm. Practise 3, 3, 3. Keep the 1 and 2 fingers on the strings. Then practise 1 2 3, 1 2 3, then 3 2 1, 3 2 1. Put all three fingers back in a group before you play the first note of each group.

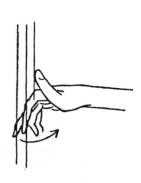

When you are comfortable working with this finger, try Lesson Two.

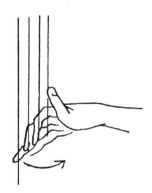

4th Finger

Since the 4th is shorter than the others, you will find that you may have to space your fingers out on the strings a little as you put this one on the G. You will probably have to bend your 2 and 3 fingers slightly so that the 4th is the only finger which goes on completely straight. The plucking action is the same - downwards, ending up bent into palm. Practise 4 4 4. Keep 1 2 3 on strings. Practise 1 2 3 4, 1 2 3 4, 1 2 3 4, then 4 3 2 1, 4 3 2 1, 4 3 2 1. Put all four back in a group before you pluck each in turn. When not being used, fingers should be tucked into palm in a relaxed position. The little finger will usually move in sympathy with the 4th. Keep the hands relaxed. Don't bend back at the wrist.

Remember this is a strong movement.

This is not.

Spacing the fingers down the strings also avoids finger buzz where the string you have just plucked hits the next-door finger.

Setting or Placing

Good fingering technique depends on "setting" or "placing". This means that the fingers are put onto the strings in groups which take care of 3 or 4 notes at a time. You have to think ahead a little to work out whether you need perhaps two fingers above the note you are on in order to play the two higher following notes, and whether it is better to change fingers (shift) on a long note when you will have a little more time. This means that you very rarely play one note at a time without having a couple of fingers set on ready to play the next notes. It makes you feel much more secure, and improves the tone.

I have marked each of the early tunes with brackets above the fingering, indicating where to shift. All the required notes contained in the next bracket should be placed or set on at one time, ready to be played.

Finding Your Way Around the Clarsach

So many strings can look a bit daunting! Begin to familiarise yourself with one string at a time.

* <u>C</u> is a red string.

1. Using your 2nd finger play all the C's from the top of the harp to the lowest one.
2. Play all the C's from the lowest one on your harp to the highest.
3. Play all the C's in any order you like. This time play them with your thumb. Tuck your other fingers neatly into your palm and pluck with the side of the thumb.
4. Play all the C's with your RH 2nd finger, then your LH 2nd finger. Then with the RH thumb then the LH thumb.

* <u>F</u> is a black or blue string.

1. Using your RH 2nd finger, play all the F's from the highest to the lowest. If your harp has metal wound strings at the bottom, the F will be slightly darker than the other strings.
2. Play all the F's from the lowest to the highest.
3. Play all the F's in any order. Use your RH 2nd finger, then LH 2nd finger. Then RH thumb, then LH thumb.

* 1. Put your RH thumb on a C. The next string down is <u>B.</u> Put your 2nd finger on that, play it, keeping your thumb in place on the C.
2. Find the other B's from the top to the bottom of your harp.
3. Play them with RH 2nd finger, then LH 2nd finger, then RH thumb, then LH thumb.

* 1. Put your RH thumb on an F. The next string down is <u>E.</u> Put your 2nd finger on that and play it, keeping your thumb in place on the F.
2. Find all the other E's on your harp.
3. Play them with 2nd and 1st (thumb) in both hands.

* 1. Put your RH 2nd finger on C. The next string up is <u>D.</u> Put your thumb on it, and play it, keeping 2nd in place.
2. Find all the other D's.
3. Play them with 2nd and 1st (thumb) in both hands.

* 1. Put your RH second finger on F. The next string up is <u>G.</u> Put your 1st (thumb) on it and play it, keeping 2nd in place.
2. Find all the G's on your harp.
3. Play them with 2nd and 1st in both hands.

* 1. The last string, half way between the red C and the black F, is <u>A.</u> Find all the A's.
2. Play them with 2nd and 1st in both hands.

Practise finding each string till you can go straight onto the one you want.

Lesson One – **Two Fingers**

I have given all the exercises nonsense titles which fit their rhythm.

Stepping Up and Stepping Down.

E♭ tuning   AEB levers
C tuning   no levers

All the bells are ringing loudly

Try these with two fingers in the same hand. Set both fingers on the strings at a time.

Rock between the two fingers. Put one back before you play the other.

Get used to the safe feeling of setting two fingers on the strings before you play each pair. Try to play it smoothly. Putting your fingers on firmly will lessen any buzz as they touch the strings.

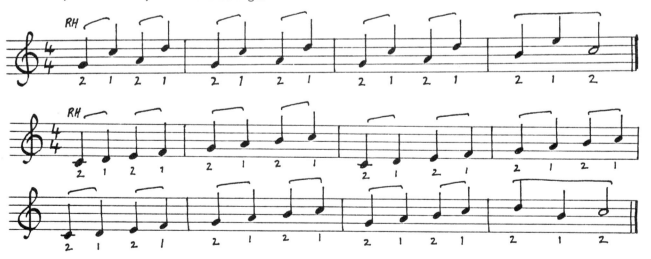

Play them with the left hand on its own

Play them with both hands together, an octave apart.

26.

1. The Fairy Lullaby

E♭ tuning AEB levers
C tuning no levers

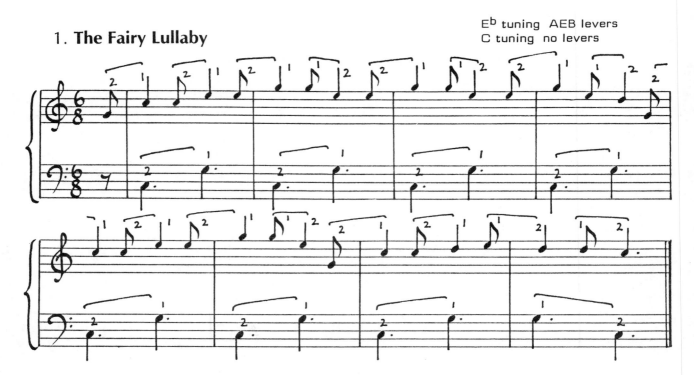

In this tune your fingers will move in pairs so that every time you shift you will "set" two fingers on. It is important to get the feeling of this "setting" ahead. It will make you feel much more secure.

Try playing the melody with the left hand. Play it an octave lower. Use the same fingering. It is a good idea to make your left hand work as hard as your right.

Play them together in octaves for practice. Try putting in a simple bass line. Set the 2 and 1 on C and G. You will pluck one then the other. Try to put each finger back just as you play the next note. It feels as if you are rocking to and fro. You will always have at least one finger on the strings. Practise it on its own till it feels safe.

Can you play the right hand with that?

2. The Christ Child's Lullaby

E♭ AEB levers
C tuning no levers

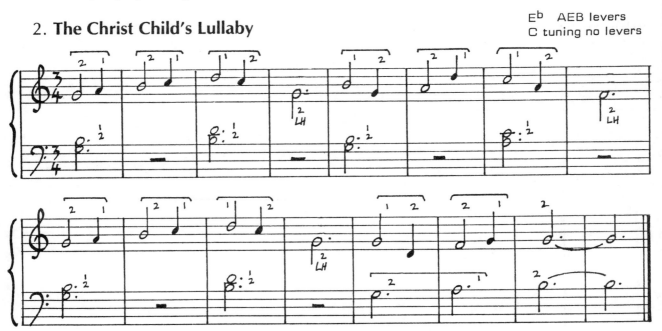

27.

Lesson Two — **Three Fingers**

When I can play I will not have to stop

E♭ AEB levers
C tuning no levers

Only play the treble line until you can play it comfortably with right hand or left hand. Do the same for all the exercises. Then add in the bass line when you feel confident about the melody.

Roundabout, roundabout, roundabout spin at the fairground tonight

Try to put the 3rd finger on just before you play the thumb. Get a feeling of a circular rocking movement

28.

Every morning I ride my motorbike, every morning I ride it

Practise the top line with right hand alone then left hand alone, then both hands in octaves. Then try the bass line.

3. Hush a ba birdie

E♭ tuning AEB levers
C tuning no levers

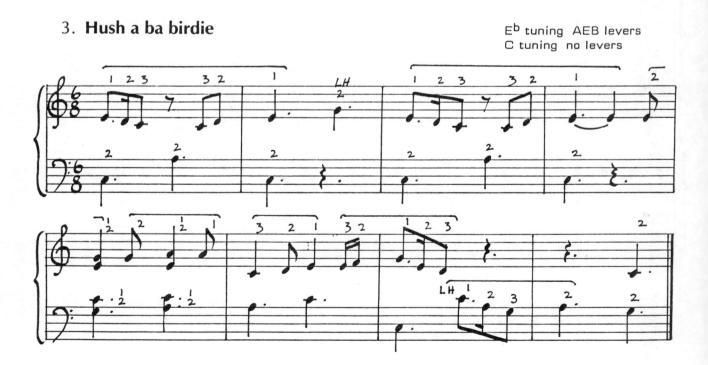

29.

4. Katie Bairdie

E♭   AEB levers
C tuning no levers

In the fourth part the left hand comes up and plays every second harmony note above the right hand. The right hand keeps playing as before.

You can play all the parts together if you get together with a few other harp players.

Lesson Three – **Triad Chords**

Eᵇ tuning – AEB levers
C tuning – no levers

Triads are a chord made up of three equally spaced notes. The first note, third and fifth of the chord are used. They can start on any note, and can be played in any octave on your clarsach.

Get the feel of the hand position for both of these basic chords. Many tunes are based on them. Play them all over your harp so that your fingers go straight onto them comfortably.

Flowing down the river.

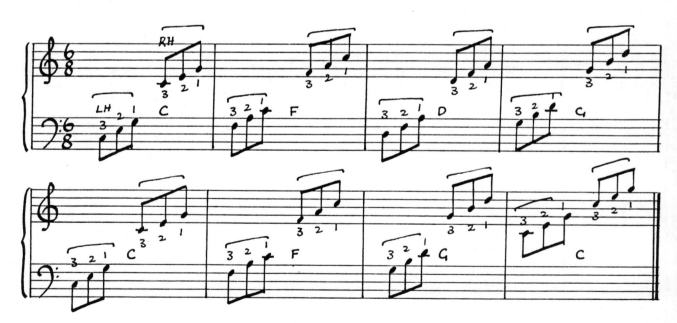

31.

5. Hey ca' thru'

E♭ tuning AEB levers
C tuning no levers

32.

Up wi the carles o' Dysart An' the lads o' Buckhe'en, A' the kimmers o' Largo
An' the lasses o' Leven

Hey ca' thru, ca' thru for we hae mickle a do. Hey ca' thru, ca' thru for we hae
mickle a do.

We hae tales tae tell
An' we hae sangs tae sing
We hae pennies tae spend
An' we hae pints tae bring
    Hey ca' thru ...

We'll live a' oor days
An' them that come behin'
Let them dae the same
And spend the gear they win
    Hey ca' thru ...

Words by Robert Burns

You can play the parts separately, or together if you have more than one harp
player. The fourth part also works well as a song accompaniment, so I have
included the words.

33.

6. The Battle's O'er

E♭ tuning AEB levers
C tuning no levers

Get both hands working on the tune

Listen to how the bass note rings on making a drone chord to accompany the tune. Play it nice and loud!

Lesson Four – **Four Fingers**

Little Baby Don't Cry

E♭   AEB levers
C tuning no levers

The basic chord is doh-mi-soh-doh. You can turn it round (inversions) by re-arranging these notes

You can play all these chords when your harp is tuned in C.

Basic 4 note
Chord positions   Inversions

In a garden grows a tree

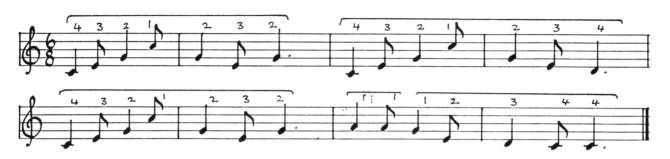

Scales with two hands

C/MAJOR

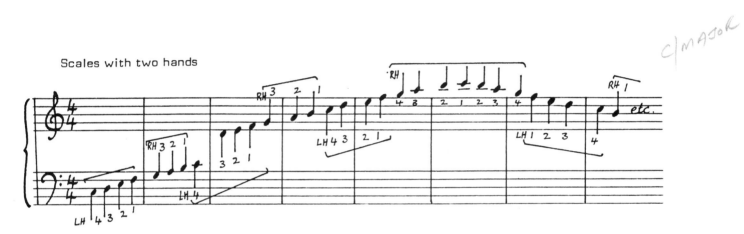

Set L.H. and R.H. in place to start. Play the four L.H. notes. Then, as you play the R.H. notes, set the L.H. in place for its next four notes. Practice until you feel your hands setting the groups of notes on neatly, with no pauses as you shift between hands.

Arpeggio with two hands   Everyone's favourite

Play the left hand then, before you play the right hand, set left hand position ready for its turn. If your harp has a wide range you can start an octave lower. But use the same fingering 4 3 2 1, 3 2 1, 3 2 1, etc. Try playing arpeggios starting on different notes. You always play the 1st note, 3rd, 5th and octave notes.

7. Over the Sea to Skye

E♭ tuning AEB levers
C tuning no levers

This is a very well known tune that you may enjoy playing. Because it is a traditional tune, the arrangement includes two different "grace-notes" or decorations. These are little notes which are written small and linked to the main melody notes. They don't take up any time, and are played very quickly. Set the necessary fingers back on the strings before you play them, as shown in the brackets above the music. The most important note is always the melody note.

I have fingered it so that you may leave out the grace-notes till you have mastered the first Decoration Exercises, if you like. But try them - they're not difficult!

Lesson Five – **Crossing under, crossing over**

Scales

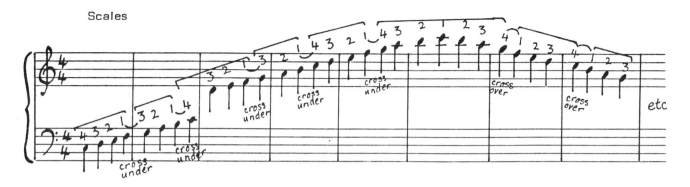

When you get to the thumb, before you play it, cross the 3rd finger underneath and place it on the next string. Then play the thumb, and set all the other fingers you need on the strings.

Crossing down the scale, use the same fingering. Thumb cross over onto the next string before you play the last finger of the set group

Arpeggios

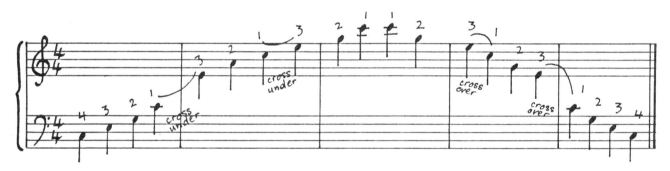

Play it with right hand and left hand separately, then together in octaves.

In the last descending run, before you play the 3 finger, cross the thumb over the top and place it on the next string down. This is why you must keep thumbs up and fingers pushed down

Going down the rocky road to Inverbervie Bay.

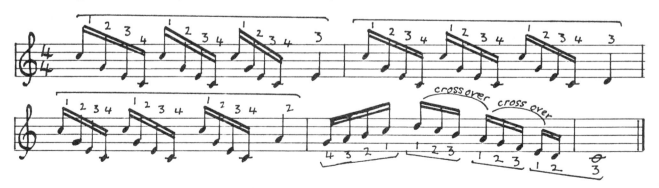

8. Fiona's gone to Broughty Ferry

Alison Kinnaird

E♭ AEB levers
C tuning no levers

39.

Lesson Six – **Moving Around your harp**

Thumb slides

Place your thumb on C in a good upright position. Fingers gathered in a relaxed bunch in your palm.

Slide the thumb onto the next string. Let the weight of your hand do the work, don't push it.

Slide with third

Set 1 2 3 4 on for each group. Slide the thumb as you pluck each of the lower fingers.

Play it with both hands separately, then together in octaves

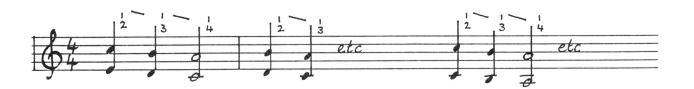

Try sliding the thumb with 2 3 4 playing a 6th below   or an octave

9. Miss A. Kingsnorth of Temple

Alison Kinnaird

E♭ tuning AEB levers
C tuning no levers

E♭ tuning – AEBF levers
C tuning – F lever

10. Islay Jig

Alan Reid Arr. Alison Kinnaird

Note that the F♯ is needed here for the key of G so we have a different pattern of levers.

42.

ORNAMENTATION AND DECORATION

One of the main differences between traditional style playing and classical playing is that the traditional musician is free to decorate the melody and is <u>expected</u> to decorate it, with little grace-notes of his own choice. This gives the musician a chance to express the tune in his own personal way, and can add a great deal of interest and individuality to it. (This does occur, in a rather different form, in one or two particular styles of classical music, like Baroque music). On the clarsach it also performs the important function of creating an on-going shimmer of harmony around the melody because of the ringing nature of the instrument. By giving many interesting harmonic possibilities which fit the traditional character of the tunes, it also gives a guide as to which notes to play in the bass line. Classical rules of harmony do not always apply to traditional music and we have no real idea as to how the harpers accompanied the basic harp melodies which have survived. I therefore find it useful to decorate the melody to begin with, and then fit the bass harmony in with that.

Where to Decorate

It is impossible to teach people <u>where</u> to put decoration into a melody. It is very much a matter of personal taste. There are still some regional differences surviving, for example a singer from Lewis will decorate more than a singer from Skye. Scottish music tends to be slightly less decorated than Irish, and we would use different decorations in different places. The <u>only</u> way to learn where to do it is to listen as often as possible to fiddle players, pipers, singers and whistle players. Your ear will gradually pick up the style. Listening to other musicians is also the only way to learn the timing and emphasis of the decorations. The musical notation is only a rough guide and really cannot reproduce it accurately. I have often heard musicians, reading from printed music, play decoration completely out of character with traditional music though they are playing exactly what is written. The <u>only</u> way, and I cannot stress this enough, is to listen to other traditional musicians. This is where the continuity and strength of the oral tradition survives. It is also much <u>easier</u> to learn the intricate grace-notes aurally than from printed music!

Basic Guidelines

The melody notes are always more important than the decoration.

The decoration should not interrupt the melodic flow or rhythm of the music.

If you find a particular grace-note gets in the way, do not play it, or change it for another one. However, I have fingered all the decoration in these arrangements so that they are as convenient as possible. Please don't take all the decoration out.

Do not learn fingering for an undecorated melody and then try to add in decoration. You will have to relearn a different fingering as you decorate it on the harp.

Only put in a few simple decorations to start with. Over elaboration is as bad, or worse, than none at all. Only add graces where you feel the tune really needs them.

SIMPLE ORNAMENTATION

E♭ tuning - AEBF levers
C tuning - F lever

For this we will use the melody of the Fairy Lullaby. This is set in the key of G this time. The reason for this is that we will not play any coloured strings throughout the exercises.

If you are not an experienced player, just work on the first three decorations – Cuts, Doublets and Running Triplets. These are the most commonly used graces. The other decorations can be attempted by more advanced players, when you feel ready for them.

1. The Cut

Use two fingers for each pair of notes. Shift where the brackets indicate. The grace-note is very light. It does not take up any time value and the melody note should always be played more strongly than the grace-note. I have put a cut onto each main melody note as an exercise but of course in a tune properly played you would not decorate every note, especially with the same grace-note.

2. The Doublet

The doublet consists of two notes played before the main melody note. They either rise or fall, depending on which way the melody is going.

This is where you have quite a choice of the notes you can play. You can choose any two notes, except C or F. I set this exercise in G to make it easier to see the choice. As a rough guide, if a note does not occur in the melody, it very often should not be included in the harmony either. There are very interesting harmonic possibilities even in just the first bar.

Choices

Listen to the way the grace-notes ring on, creating a harmony. The melody note must always be the most important one. Grace-notes have no time value. Try out all the possible harmonies on each doublet.

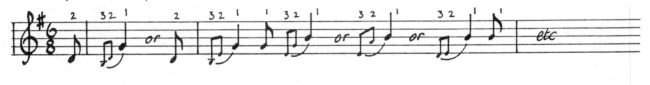

3. Running Triplets – One on each beat for practice.

Running Triplets follow the same pattern as Doublets, except that you are adding three notes in front of each main melody note. The grace-notes should again be very lightly played, and should not interrupt the flow of the tune. The harmonic effects are beautiful. You can choose any three notes before the melody note in this tune except C or F.

For example in the first bar.

MORE DECORATION

Eb tuning - AEBF levers
C tuning - F lever

4. <u>Shakes</u> - In the Shake you rock very quickly between the 2 and thumb. The grace-notes are so quick that they are hardly perceptible. The melody notes must be strongest. Again you can choose a diferent note for the second grace-note, though the first note is always the same as the melody note. No C's or F's.

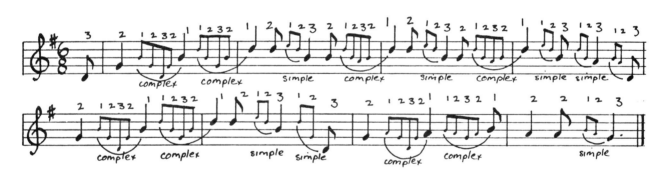

5. <u>Turns - Complex and Simple</u>

The function of "turns" is to link two notes, rising or descending. The second finger is set on the melody note so that the 1 and 3 are available to play one note higher and one note lower. Complex turns link rising notes, simple turns look much like doublets but, while doublets can be played on any note, a simple turn will always link two descending notes.

MORE COMPLICATED DECORATION

Eᵇ tuning - ABEF levers
C tuning - F lever

6. Throw or Grip

The Throw or Grip is a pipe style grace where the three grace-notes are played very fast before the melody note. Listen to pipers to hear how they should be played. You can experiment with the harmonic effects possible by varying the two notes played by 1 and 3. 2 always goes on the melody note, and plays strongest.

7. Triplet on one note

This is rather a slow melody on which to do this decoration, but it gives a good idea of how it functions. Fingers 4 3 2 play the same string in turn, very fast. You will find that you have to turn the fingers in slightly and play more on their tips. It is as much a rhythmic effect as part of the melody, and occurs very often in dance music.

COMPOSITE DECORATIONS

Played with Two Hands

8. I really like this decoration because it sets up a drone chord which echoes throughout the tune, but is still rhythmically intesting. Think of the four notes before each beat as a single rhythmic entity (a-ya-ta-ta-tum).

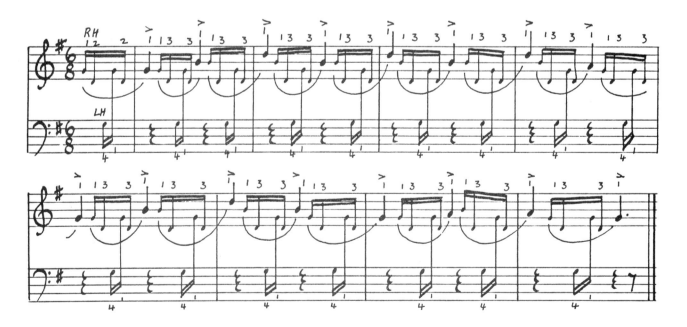

9. Again this decoration should take up hardly any time at all. It's more of a rhythmic 'gurgle' before each melody note. Note how the first note of the grace-notes changes to follow the melody.

11. The Kilbarchan Weaver

Alison Kinnaird

E♭ tuning AEB levers
C tuning no levers

12. The Atholl Highlanders

E^b tuning   AEBF levers
C tuning   F levers

50.

13. Kenmure's up and awa'

E♭ tuning   AEBF levers
C tuning   F levers

March

51.

14. Farewell to Glenshalloch *(Bothan an Easan)*

Eb Tuning   AEBFC levers

C tuning   FC levers

Flowing

52.

15. Queen Elizabeth's March

P.-M. W. Ross

Arr. A. Kinnaird

E^b Tuning AEBFC levers

C tuning   FC levers

16. Iain Beag *(Little John)*

Alison Kinnaird

E♭ Tuning AEBFC levers
C tuning   FC levers

Flowing

17. An Argyllshire Air – Ossian's Daydream

E^b tuning AEB levers
C tuning no levers

18. Cro Cinn t-Saile *(The Cattlefold of Kintail)*

Eᵇ tuning   AEBF levers
C tuning   F levers

56.

19. Drops of Brandy

20. Brose and Butter

57.

21. Balfour Village

Bob Groat   Arr. A. Kinnaird

E♭Tuning AEBFC levers

C tuning FC levers

Polka

22. The Shapinsay Polka

John Sinclair   Arr. A. Kinnaird

E♭ Tuning   AEBFC levers
C tuning· FC levers

23. **Sae Mirrie as we have Bein**

Eᵇ tuning   AEBF levers
C tuning   F levers

60.

24. Hench me, Mallie Gray

E♭ tuning AEBF levers

C tuning F levers

Brisk

RH may be played an octave higher

Repeat last 2 bars ad libitum growing fainter

61.

25. Drummond Castle

Niel Gow

Eᵇ tuning AEB levers
C tuning no levers

62.

26. Leslie's March

E♭ Tuning AEBFC levers
C tuning FC levers

63.

27. Lamentation for James Moray of Abercairney

Niel Gow

Eᵇ tuning AEBF levers

C tuning F levers

64.

28. Glenlivet

Eᵇ tuning AEB levers
C tuning no levers

65.

29. Deil amang the Tailors

E♭ tuning AEBFCG levers
C tuning FCG levers

30. The Rymer

Alison Kinnaird

E♭ tuning AEBF levers
C tuning F levers

31. **A' Bhanais Iortach** *(The St Kilda Wedding March)*

E♭ tuning AEBFCG levers

C tuning FCG levers

32. An Oidhche robh na Phosadh – The Feet Washing

E♭ tuning – no levers
C tuning – FCGD levers

69.

33. Caoineadh Eoghain Rua *(Lament for Owen Roe)*

E♭ tuning AEBF levers
C tuning F levers

70.

34. Kid on the Mountain

E♭ tuning   AEBF levers

C tuning   F levers

35. Lady Cunninghame of Livingstone

Nathaniel Gow

E♭ tuning AEBFCG levers
C tuning FCG levers

Pastorale

36. Dunkeld Steeple

Niel Gow

E♭ tuning AEBFCG levers
C tuning FCG levers

73.

G major
↓ 2
Relative E minor + #7 D#

37. Roslin Castle

Eᵇ tuning AEBF levers
C tuning F levers

74.

38. The Massacre of Glencoe 1691

Eb tuning – AEBFC levers
F tuning – FC levers

75.

39. **Caileach an Dudain** *(The Old Woman of the Mill Dust)*

40. Sleepy Maggie

Eb Tuning   AEBFC levers
C tuning   FC levers

ARRANGING MUSIC

When you are reasonably confident at playing other people's arrangements, you can start to make your own, of traditional tunes or your own compositions. In fact, if you want to play good traditional music, you <u>must</u> make your own arrangements because each performer should sound unique and be recognisably different from everyone else. If you are just beginning to arrange, however, don't worry too much about being original to start off with. If you play what pleases you, you will eventually develop an individual style.

There are some great bonuses about doing your own arrangements. First, you only need to play the tunes you like best. Second, you never need to arrange anything in a way which feels too awkward or uncomfortable. Don't worry about putting in "difficult bits" to impress other clarsach players! If you enjoy playing a tune, you will play it well, and your audience will appreciate it. In any case, when you hear someone else playing the harp it always sounds very complicated and impressive - even if you know that the tune they are playing is not very technically demanding.

Traditional music gives great scope for personal freedom and creativity. This is one of the most enjoyable things about it. There are no particular rules about arranging it, so if you are a classically trained musician, you need to think afresh about approaching traditional music without making the assumption that classical harmonies will fit. However, the fact that there are no rules does not mean that anything goes! There can be bad traditional music, as can happen in any field of music.

Here are some guidelines which I have found work successfully.

1. First - and by far the most important - listen as much as possible to good traditional musicians (playing all the different instruments, not just harp players) to attune your ear to the idiom of the music, and how they treat it. It is like learning a language with the right accent. If you do not know where to find good traditional music live, there are many fine recordings available.

2. Remember that in traditional music the melody is <u>always</u> the most important element in a tune. Decoration and harmony are of much less importance. The melody should always remain prominent.

3. Begin by getting the tune into your head so that you can recognise how it flows, and notice anything particularly interesting about the melody that you would like to bring out. Don't learn fingering for it on the harp at this point.

4. Work out any decorations that you think suit the tune. Only put in a few to begin with. Start with simple ones, like a couple of cuts, or a turn. Only add them where you think the tune needs something. They must not interrupt the flow of the melody. Too many ornamentations are as bad, or worse, than none at all.

5. Play the ornamented melody, working out a sensible fingering. Use both hands if necessary, especially in dance tunes. Make it as comfortable for yourself to play as you can. If you find one of the decorations does not fit at this point, change it or leave it out. Practise this until you can play the melody fluently.

6. Listen to the harmonies you are creating with the notes of the melody ringing together, and the harmonies made by the grace-notes.

7. Begin to add in bass harmony notes. These must fit in with the decoration. You can sometimes pick out a note you are using as a decoration and play it an octave lower as a bass harmony. Sometimes a group of grace-notes, like a triplet, will sound lovely as a chord played at the same point, again in another octave. Think of the bass line as another way of decorating the melody.

8. Listen to the melody again and decide if it needs to be "pointed" or emphasised anywhere. At this time you may work out which chords sound good along with it. Don't add a handful of notes in the basic chord pattern. Your arrangements will inevitably end up cluttered and boring.

9. Pick out one note from the chord that you like at one point. Is one note enough to support and strengthen the melody? If not, add in the same note an octave lower or higher. Is that enough? If not, add in another note, perhaps the 5th. If you like that, leave it in. If not, try another note, maybe the 3rd or 4th. At each point ask yourself if that is enough in the way of harmony. If you feel it is getting cluttered or the melody is getting lost, leave some harmony out.

10. When you have decided on the ornamentation, the harmonies that suit the ornamentation, and the strong bass harmonies, listen again and see if the tune needs anything more added to it. It may not, or it may sound a little bare at some point so you might add in a couple of single harmony notes to fill it out. Again, be aware of the ringing nature of the instrument. The notes resound for a long time and you should aim to play as few notes at a time as necessary.

11. If you can think of another way in which you would like to express the melody, change the arrangement when you play it through for a second time. You may change the ornamentation or the harmony, or both. A simple way to change it is to play a tune once in a high octave, and then an octave lower. This is particularly effective with slow airs.

Suggestions

* Playing the melody in octaves with two hands makes it very strong. This is useful for short passages.

* Where you have a run of melody notes ascending in thirds, try playing the same notes decending in the left hand at the same time. Thirds, fourths or fifths following the melody or running counter to it often work well for a sequence of notes.

* If you are not sure which harmony to use, try decorating the melody note and then use those notes for a left hand chord. You find some unusual and beautiful harmonies this way.

* Try to think of a counter melody (a tune you can play along with the melody for a few bars or a whole part of a tune). Chords become very boring all the time.

* If you are playing a melody along with someone else, put your decorations in a different place from theirs, sometimes. This makes it much more interesting.

* Try playing broken chords downwards for a change. It is said that the old harpers always broke their chords downwards. It emphasises the melody note more and, since it is not much used in classical music, gives a different feel to the harmony.

* I rarely play the third note in important chords. The octave and fifth give a stronger effect and, since they are more used with the pipes and fiddle, fit in with a traditional sound well.

* If one chord occurs frequently in a tune, which often happens, it tends to become boring. Make it more interesting by playing single notes out of it, perhaps in different octaves. Play them also in an unusual order - e.g. instead of 'doh' note, third, fifth, octave, try 'doh', octave, fifth, octave, third. This is often useful at the end of a tune instead of a plain broken chord.

* If the tune is a dance tune, think how you can best bring out the rhythm. This should obviously be steady, but you can vary the harmony rhythm to make it more interesting by, for example, playing one strong chord on the beat, nothing but melody for a few bars, then coming in again with the bass at a significant point. Scottish music also lends itself quite often to a syncopated beat, but use restraint - too much of that loses the surprise element!

Things To Avoid

* Don't set up a rhythm in the left hand, like running arpeggios, that you will find hard to stop. If you do this you will find yourself following the harmony rhythm with your melody, regularising it. The harmony should always support but be secondary to the melody. This is particularly important with slow airs.

* Bass drones. Many Scottish and Irish tunes are based on a drone harmony. This does not mean that you have to play it on the first beat of every bar! This is one of the cliches of arrangers who know nothing about Scottish music. Play one of your bass strings and listen to how long it resounds. This will carry through several bars of music and only needs to be played again at significant points where you want emphasis.

* Avoid playing too many notes at once in a chord. The ringing strings make the sound very muddy. You should be able to hear every note - or else they should be left out.

I have written out some tunes that would fit well on the clarsach. Have a go at making your own arrangement - and enjoy yourself!

The Canty Auld Man - Jig

Lord Haddo's Favourite - Slow Air

Miss McLeod's Minuet

The Man With Two Women   - Reel

83.

Braigh Loch Iall - Slow Air

Skint O' Siller - Reel

NOTES

Many tunes have interesting stories behind them. You should always try to find out about their background. It makes it much more interesting for your audience, and yourself – and you will play them better if you know what the tunes are about.

1. The Fairy Lullaby

One of the duties of the harper was to play the clan to sleep at night, and lullabies are certainly particularly effective on the clarsach. This is the melody of a well-known song, the words of which are sung by a mother searching for her child, which seems to have been stolen by the fairies. Stories of the fairies stealing or leaving their own changelings in place of human children are quite common, but the picturesque legends conceal a less romantic reality – the parents of an unwanted or malformed child would sometimes abandon it on a hillside, or even murder it, saying that it had been taken by the fairies.

2. The Christ Child's Lullaby

This is the tune of a Gaelic hymn, often sung at Christmas. The chorus is simply "Halleluia", repeated over and over, with one syllable to each bar.

3. Hush A Ba Birdie

A little Scots lullaby that my mother used to sing to us. The words are:

> Hush a ba birdie, croon, croon,
> Hush a ba birdie, croon,
> The sheep are gane to the silver wood,
> And the cows are all gane to the broom, broom
>
> O it's braw milking the kye, kye,
> O it's braw milking the kye,
> The birds are singing, the bells are ringing,
> And the wild deer come galloping by, by
>
> Hush a ba birdie, croon, croon,
> Hush a ba birdie, croon,
> The gaits are gane to the mountains high,
> And they'll no be hame until noon, noon.

4. Katie Bairdie

Another Scots nursery rhyme telling about the animals in Katie Bairdie's farmyard.

> Katie Bairdie had a coo,
> Black and white aboot the moo,
> Wasna that a daintie coo,
> Dance Katie Bairdie.

5. Hey Ca' Thru'

Robert Burns is said to have written the words for this song about the fisher folk of Fife. He was one of the great folksong collectors of his day, and collected many traditional tunes, often writing words to them in order to preserve them.

6. The Battle's O'er

A slow march for the pipes.

7. Over the Sea to Skye

One of the best known Scottish songs. The words which link it with Bonnie Prince Charlie and Flora MacDonald are probably of much more recent origin than the melody.

8. **Fiona's Gone to Broughty Ferry**

    A tune written for a pupil, who was moving house to near Dundee.

9. **Miss A. Kingsnorth of Temple**

    I often compose tunes for my pupils, which are really thinly disguised exercises! It makes practising much more fun if you have your own tune. Why don't you make one up for yourself or a member of your own family?

10. **Islay Jig**

    Alan Reid of Battlefield Band wrote this tune when we were working on some film music. I found that it fits very well on the harp. You can play it quite slow, or in jig time.

11. **The Kilbarchan Weaver**

    I composed this tune for 'Held In Trust', a film series on the National Trust for Scotland. This tune was to accompany the movement of a hand loom in the weaver's cottage at Kilbarchan, which is owned by the National Trust.

12. **The Atholl Highlanders**

    A well-known pipe march. The Duke of Atholl is the only person in Britain allowed to keep his own private army - though it only consists of a few men and a small pipe band, and now just appears on ceremonial occasions.

13. **Kenmure's Up And Awa'**

    This is another pipe march. It dates from at least 1715 when Jacobite words were set to it supporting William, Viscount Kenmure, who led the forces of King James in the south of Scotland. You can play tunes 12 and 13 one after the other.

14. **Farewell to Glenshalloch/Bothan An Easan**

    A lovely slow air from R.A. Smith's "The Scotish Minstrel". James Hogg wrote rather romantic Jacobite words to it some time after the actual Risings. The tune is probably a lot older. Glenshalloch is near Ullapool, in Wester Ross, and is most notable for the spectacularly deep Corryshalloch Gorge, now owned by the National Trust for Scotland.

15. **Queen Elizabeth's March**

    This is a modern pipe march composed by Pipe Major William Ross, who was Pipe Major at Edinburgh Castle. You should listen to some pipe music so that you know how to play the grace-notes.

16. **Iain Beag (Little John)**

    I made up this tune for our son, John. It is a good one for practising triads or chords in the left hand. Watch out for the bar which is double the length of the others in the middle of the second part.

17. **An Argyleshire Air (Ossian's Daydream)**

    This beautiful slow air is found, untitled, in Patrick Macdonald's Collection which dates from the mid 18th century. The name of Ossian, the bard of the Fianna has become linked with it, but this was probably part of the romantic enthusiasm for all things Celtic during the 19th century. Marjory Kennedy-Fraser also published English words to it.

18. **Cro Cinn t-Saile (The Cattlefold of Kintail)**

This tune is well-known as an exile's song with the bard wishing to return to his home in Kintail, and also in a slightly different variant as "The Mackenzie Lullaby" which was said to have been sung to the children of the Mackenzies of Seaforth.

19. **Drops of Brandy**

20. **Brose and Butter**

Two 9/8 jigs which you can play following each other. The first is well known in Ireland as well as in Scotland. "Brose and Butter" is linked with King Charles II. It was said to be his favourite tune, and that it was often played for him by his friend, the Laird of Cockpen (hero of the song) who followed the King into exile when he lost his Crown, and in doing so forfeited all his lands. When the King came into his own again the Laird tried to get an audience with him to regain his property, but no-one would let him see the King. So he found out where the King was going to church and asked the organist to let him play during the service. But no-one noticed his playing until, in desperation, as the King was leaving the Laird struck up this tune "Brose and Butter" which, not surprisingly, caught the King's attention. He probably didn't process down the aisle in jig time too often! So he found his long lost friend and restored his fortune. A good story!

21. **Balfour Village**

22. **The Shapinsay Polka**

These are two charming polkas from Shapinsay, one of the Orkney Isles. They are modern tunes, the first composed by Bob Groat and the second composed by John Sinclair, both of whom are fine fiddle players, and kindly gave me permission to arrange and publish their tunes in this book. You can play them one after the other. The fiddle is, of course, the main instrument in Orkney and there is no tradition of using the clarsach there, but the tunes flow delightfully on the harp. I hope you will enjoy playing them as much as I do myself.

23. **Sae Mirrie As We Have Bein**

This is a lute tune from the 17th century Straloch M.S. The lute took over many tunes that were played on the harp and, because they were written down by members of the aristocracy and court musicians, they survived when the harp died out. I have no reason to think that this tune was composed for the harp, but it is a lovely melody. You can play it and go into the next tune.

24. **Hench Me, Mallie Gray**

Another lute tune - rather an odd tune, in fact, but great fun to play. It should be played forcefully, at a brisk marching speed. Do play right hand and left hand notes where I suggest. It is the only way to get the neat, clipped rhythm. I don't know what the title means, but I suspect it's rude!

25. **Drummond Castle**

This is a Niel Gow jig with a good bouncy rhythm. As usual, I have fingered it so that the strongest fingers 1 and 2 play the important notes most of the time. Keep the time steady and don't play too fast - more dance tunes have been ruined by people thinking that "faster" means "better" - it doesn't! Drummond Castle is in Strathearn in Perthshire. It was built by the 1st Lord Drummond in 1487, and is still inhabited by his descendants.

26. **Leslie's March**

This is another march called after General Sir David Leslie, who commanded the Covenanters' forces, first against Montrose, who was fighting for Charles II, and then, when the Covenanters decided to support Charles, against Cromwell, who defeated Leslie at Dunbar in 1650.

27. **Lamentation for James Moray of Abercairney**

Niel Gow (1727-1807) was the most famous Highland fiddle player. He was born near Dunkeld in Perthshire. His main patron was the Duke of Atholl but this beautiful lament was composed on the death of one of his other patrons, James Moray. It is interesting that Niel Gow's mother, whose maiden name was MacEwan, may have been descended from the MacEwans who were honorary harpers to the Atholl family for hundreds of years. Certainly many Gow tunes fit beautifully on the clarsach.

28. **Glenlivet**

A reel which I find fits well after the previous tune. Remember to turn one of the F blades.

29. **Deil Among The Tailors**

Another well-known reel. Don't play it too fast!

30. **The Rymer**

I composed this tune and named it after Thomas the Rymer – True Tammas – a historical character who lived in the 15th century and who made many prophecies about the area in which I live, in the Borders. He is the subject of many legends and ballads telling of how he received his gift of always telling the truth from the Faery Queen.

31. **A' Bhanais Iortach (The St. Kilda Wedding March)**

This tune comes from the Simon Fraser Collection and has been played by many of the folk bands. St. Kilda, which is an isolated group of rocky islands far to the west of the Scottish mainland, was evacuated in the 1930's as the life there was thought too harsh for its inhabitants. In the past, however, it seems to have been rich at least in music, and there are a surprising number of fine Gaelic songs and tunes which have come down to us from such a small community.

32. **An Oidhche robh na 'Phosadh (The Feet Washing)**

Staying on a wedding theme, this is another tune from the Simon Fraser Collection. The title in English is not a translation of the Gaelic, which means "The Night of the Wedding", but Fraser explains that washing the feet was an important part of the nuptial celebrations.

33. **Caoineadh Eoghain Rua (The Lament for Owen Roe)**

I learned this tune from my husband, Robin Morton. It is Irish and a lament for either Owen Roe O'Neill, a soldier, or Owen Roe O'Sullivan – Owen of the Sweet Mouth – who was a famous poet. The timing is very free, and impossible to write with a regular time signature, or even fixed bar lines. It is an exceptionally beautiful and powerful tune, and though the harmony notes are very few, it needs great care and sensitive handling.

34. **Kid on the Mountain**

This Irish slip-jig follows "Owen Roe" very well. I like the change into the minor key, which sounds exciting. Like most dance tunes, the speed is much better controlled, then the tune has drive rather than running away with you.

35. Lady Cunninghame of Livingstone

This pastorale (it's a bit quicker than a slow air) was composed by Nathaniel Gow, Niel's son. It is a beautiful example of an 18th century fiddle tune with its elegant construction. Nathaniel, who lived from 1766-1831, was taken up by London society and often played with great success at Almack's and the other fashionable London clubs.

36. Dunkeld Steeple

Niel Gow composed this tune to honour the bells of Dunkeld, near where he was born. The bell-like phrases suit the clarsach beautifully, so remember to let them ring like bells. I learned this version from Brian McNeill of Battlefield Band, and have since found out that it's not exactly the way Gow wrote it - but I like this one better!

37. Roslin Castle

This slow air is typical of the fiddle airs of the early 19th century. It is romantic and rather brooding, which suits the subject. Roslin Castle is now an impressive ruin over-looking Roslin Glen in an historic part of Midlothian. You need to be neat with your blade or lever change.

38. The Massacre of Glencoe 1691

The tragedy caught the Scottish imagination and it is not surprising that there are many songs and tunes about it. It wasn't so much that the Campbells massacred the Macdonalds - that happened all the time - but that they did it while in their houses as guests, which was regarded as a sacred trust. The Macdonalds promptly went over the hills to Argyll and wiped out several times as many Campbells. However, this is a romantic tune - have a picture of Glencoe in a storm in your mind's eye while you play it!

39. Caileach an Dudain (The Old Woman of the Mill Dust)

This tune was used for a very old dance. The words which were sung to it have survived though the dance has not, and the tune is now played on the pipes. You must be very neat with the grace-notes, as usual in dance tunes. As it is quite a long tune, having six parts, I find it is exciting to play and should build up to quite a climax. Play it loud!

40. Sleepy Maggie

This tune is known in Scotland and Ireland in many versions, under the titles of "Sleepy Maggie" or "Drowsy Maggie". I got this version in Oswald's Caledonian Pocket Companion (1746-59) and like this arrangement because it brings in the inherent syncopation that you find in many Scottish tunes.